MW00893668

To

_____

with all my heart!

One heart

The idea for this book came from a letter I wrote to my daughter when she was only two years old. Since the relationship between a mother and a daughter at around the time of adolescence often goes through hell and high water, I wanted her to remember that, no matter what, I would always be there beside her, her guardian angel, her greatest supporter. Along the way, I realised that I was also speaking about my own mother and that I was finally acknowledging the fact that she had always been there by my side in my times of joy and sorrow and distress.

I therefore dedicate this book to the long sequence of women who alternate in the role of mother and daughter. As the years go by, we realise how much strength we derive from our mothers, we understand that they have bequeathed to us values and habits that we had never appreciated and which, even more often, we had never acknowledged. This is a book about everything we would like to say to our daughters and to our mothers, yet often put off for another time, a time that never comes…

To Rena and Vaya from the heart….

Marina Gioti

Darling,
my heart beat like

the day you were born,
It did not take too long...

...for it to happen
– something no one had managed to do so far:
For you to steal my heart for ever, my little star,
so it would beat inside your chest from that day on,

And it was

love

that took its place.
Innocent, like nothing I had known.
Spurring every sentiment with its infinity and grace.

Your little heart now beats for two
from that day on, a single beat.
Therefore, my love, take double care. Once

for you

once also for me, my sweet.

For when you cry,
it is I who hurts and fills with tears.

When you are cross,
storms rise inside me and I am broken,
pierced with spears.

You are disappointed,
and the world around us is painted grey,
is covered by a cloud.

And when you are scared,
our one heart is crumpled,
like a paper shroud.

Yet when you laugh, I dance, amongst the fairest flowers, yearlong.

 Your every dream

 I make into wishes,

and into song.

Your every breath becomes for me
a reason for a beautiful life.

Do not forget,

I shall always be there by your side.

And when one day I will no longer be able
to be there with you,
know that I will always live
in your heart anew.

And when you cry...

...and when you laugh...

...when you are scared
and in your fears you feel lost...

...I shall be there,
your faithful companion, at my post.
You shall feel me
with every beating of your heart.

Until that day comes
when you too will have to do your part.
To your own baby give yourself with all our heart.

There too I will exist,
since there you will live.

Then, darling, you will understand
that a heart beats best
when, shared, it beats as more than one.

Marina Gioti Bio

Children's books and art are Marina Gioti's twin passions; passions that have found their perfect expression in her best-selling children's books. Born in Athens, Greece, Marina studied Marketing and Fine Arts at Georgetown University in Washington, D.C. followed by Communication Design at Pratt Institute in N.Y. She is the 1999 recipient of the John Peter's Publication Award and Scholarship from the N.Y. Art Directors Club and has won a Bronze Pentaward for her work in design. Her book, "Twice upon a time - Little Red Riding Hood," was voted as one of the 10 best picture books in her native Greece (2016).

Marina spends her time between Greece and the UK, writing, illustrating and giving book presentations to children and parents. She is a regular contributor to popular magazines and websites, and a member of the Greek Section of the International Board on Books for Young People (IBBY).

Amazon author page: amazon.com/author/marinagioti

© J.D. Strikis

You can contact Marina:

- marina@marinagioti.gr
- Marina Gioti
- MarinaGioti
- marina_gioti
- Marina Gioti

www.marinagioti.gr

Written and Illustrated by
© Marina Gioti, 2018. All Rights Reserved

First Edition in Greek, March 2017

Translated into English by Mika Provata-Carlone

Thank you for taking the time to read 'One Heart'
If you enjoyed it, please tell your friends or post a short
review on Amazon or Goodreads. Word of mouth is an
author's best friend and much appreciated!

Find out more about Marina and her books at
www.marinagioti.gr

Made in the USA
Las Vegas, NV
09 December 2020

12474596R10029